Coding
with Anna and Elsa

A *Frozen* Guide to Blockly

Written by Kiki Prottsman

Special thanks to Dr. AnnMarie Thomas,
Simon Tatom, and Code.org

Lerner Publications ◆ Minneapolis

Dear Educators:

Disney Learning's *Coding with Anna and Elsa: A Frozen Guide to Blockly* offers learners an engaging introduction to computer programming. This book presents coding concepts in child-friendly language, prompting readers to explore these concepts through both online and off-line activities. Step-by-step instructions are provided for every project, and children are encouraged to experiment and try different solutions. Remember, the iterative process of assembling code, seeing what it does, and making adjustments is more important than the end result. Learning to code will help your students develop persistence, as well as skills in reasoning, problem-solving, and creative thinking.

The *Frozen* project site is created by Code.org, a nonprofit organization dedicated to expanding access to computer science for all students. Code.org activities are licensed under the Creative Commons Attribution-NonCommercial-ShareAlike 4.0 International Public License and are used with permission.

Lerner Publications Company
A division of Lerner Publishing Group, Inc.
241 First Avenue North
Minneapolis, MN 55401 USA

For reading levels and more information, look up this title at www.lernerbooks.com.

Main body text set in Avenir LT Pro 45 Book 12/14.5
Typeface provided by Linotype AG.

Library of Congress Cataloging-in-Publication Data

Names: Prottsman, Kiki, author.
Title: Coding with Anna and Elsa : a Frozen guide to Blockly / by Kiki Prottsman.
Description: Minneapolis : Lerner Publications, [2019] | Audience: Ages 7–11. | Audience: Grades 4 to 6.
Identifiers: LCCN 2018016843 (print) | LCCN 2018019847 (ebook) | ISBN 9781541532670 (eb pdf) | ISBN 9781541532663 (lb : alk. paper) | ISBN 9781541533004 (pb : alk. paper) | ISBN 9781541532670 (ebook)
Subjects: LCSH: Blockly (Computer programming language)—Juvenile literature. | Computer programming—Juvenile literature. | Frozen (Motion picture : 2013 : Buck and Lee)
Classification: LCC QA76.73.B56 (ebook) | LCC QA76.73.B56 .P76 2019 (print) | DDC 005.13/3—dc23

LC record available at https://lccn.loc.gov/2018016843

Manufactured in the United States of America
1-44852-35722-4/18/2018

Contents

Why Code?

Learning to write **code** opens the door to a world of possibilities! When you write code, you use a special language to talk directly to a computer or machine. Code that tells computers how to complete specific tasks is called a **program**. Computer programs let you do cool things like create digital art, drive robots, and develop video games!

Coding is one part of a bigger subject called **computer science**. This is the study of computers and computer-related ideas. When you study computer science, you learn a lot of useful skills besides working with computers. You also practice problem-solving, creative thinking, teamwork, and persistence. Being persistent means that you keep trying, even when things get hard.

Professional computer programmers usually use text to write code. But we will start our lessons using a **block-based language**. Instead of text, block-based languages use code blocks that look like puzzle pieces. You drag and drop these blocks to create programs. This is a fun, easy way to learn many of the same ideas that professional programmers use! The name of the language we'll be using is **Blockly**.

The activities in this book will help you use Blockly to create some amazing drawings with your favorite *Frozen* characters. Grab a notebook and something to write with. As you work on the projects, you will break large problems into smaller pieces. This makes them much easier to solve. After some practice, you will notice challenges in the real world that you can handle the same way!

Many of the devices we use every day need code to work. Computers, phones, TVs, and even cars all use **software**. Software refers to programs that run on a machine or computer. You can't touch software, but you can see the results of it almost everywhere you go. When you use an app, see traffic signals change, or read a car's electronic display, software is at work!

A lot of the entertainment we enjoy also uses code. This includes movies, TV shows, video games, websites, and even theme park rides. Special software helps filmmakers design and animate characters in movies like *Frozen*. Code in video games tells the game how to react when the player does something. Web engineers use code to tell

computers what text and images to display when people visit their websites. And Disney Imagineers use code to program Audio-Animatronic characters, telling them how they should move and sound. As you can see, code can be used to create really amazing things!

❗ Did You Know?

❄ Computers are boxes full of circuits that shuffle electricity from one area to another. They are not smart without code. It is only through code that computers understand how to play music, show images, or run games.

Take a Tour

It's so much fun to build programs and watch them run! We will use the *Frozen* project site at Code.org to create our programs. To access the website, go to **studio.code.org/projects/frozen/.***

Are you excited to create some ice drawings with Elsa and Anna? Great! The first thing you'll need to do is learn about the space you'll be playing in. Let's take a tour of the coding website. There are three main areas to explore.

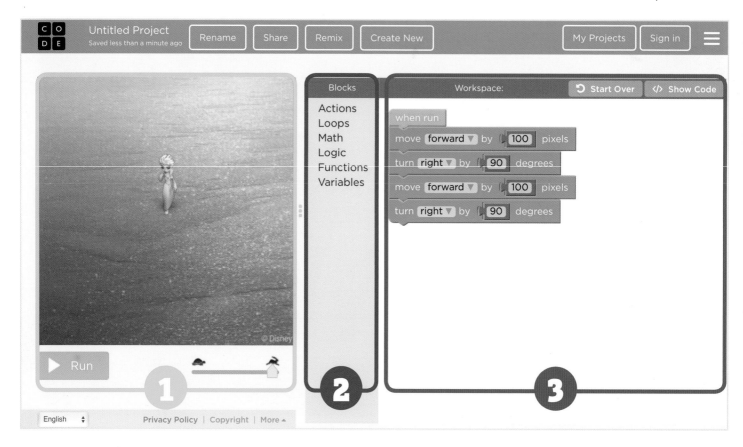

1 Play space:

This is the area where your code will run. After you've built your program, click the **Run** button to see what your code does!

2 Toolbox:

This is where all of the code blocks are stored. The blocks are organized under labels that describe the type of work they do. For example, you'll find the **move forward** block under the **Actions** label.

3 Workspace:

This is where you will build your code to make your drawings. Drag a block from the toolbox here and click it into place to add it to your program. If you want to remove any blocks, drag them back to the toolbox.

* This is not a Disney site. Disney has no responsibility for any content contained on this site or its availability.

❗ Helpful Tips

❄ If you'd like to save your projects, you need to create an account before you get started. Make sure to get an adult's permission and help.

❄ To start a new project, use the **Create New** button at the top of the page.

❄ Use the **Rename** button to give your project a name that describes what it does. Choose a fun and memorable name!

❄ After you hit the **Run** button, it becomes a **Reset** button. Use **Reset** to clear the play space and continue working on your program.

❄ Notice the slider to the right of the **Run** button. If you'd like the drawing to be completed more quickly, move the slider toward the rabbit. If you'd like the drawing to be completed more slowly, move the slider toward the turtle.

❄ The *Frozen* project site is available in many languages. The language selector is below the play space, at the bottom left. Click the button to see the available languages. Then choose the language you want.

العربية
Azərbaycan dili
български
Bosanski
Català
Čeština
Dansk
Deutsch
Ελληνικά
✓ English
Español (España)
Español (México)
▼

Let's Get Started!

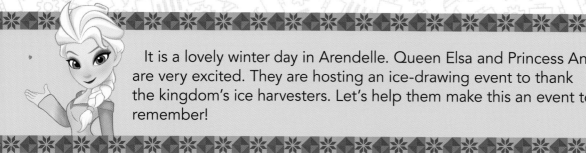

It is a lovely winter day in Arendelle. Queen Elsa and Princess Anna are very excited. They are hosting an ice-drawing event to thank the kingdom's ice harvesters. Let's help them make this an event to remember!

1 Click on the **Create New** button. This will start a new project. Use the **Rename** button to name your project "Warm-Up."

2 Help Elsa draw a straight line on the ice as she walks. First, click on the **Actions** label. Then drag a **move forward by 100 pixels** block to the workspace. Computer images are made of tiny squares of color called **pixels**. The **move forward** block tells the computer how far—how many pixels—Elsa will move. Connect it to the bottom of the **when run** block. What happens when you click the **Run** button?

3 It's hard to see the line we just drew, since Elsa is standing in front of it! Drag out a **turn right by 90 degrees** block. Slip it between the **when run** block and the **move forward by 100 pixels** block. Tap the **Reset** button. Then run your program.

4 Now let's give Anna a try! Find the **set character to Anna** block under the **Actions** label. Drag it into the workspace. Connect it between the **when run** block and the **turn right by 90 degrees** block. Click **Run** to watch Anna draw her line.

5 Anna wants to draw her line somewhere else on the ice! Grab the **jump forward by 100 pixels** block under **Actions**. Click it into your program below the **set character** block. Do you see the little arrow next to the word "forward"? Click on that, and you will see a drop-down menu with two options. Click the word "backward." Now you have a block that says **jump backward by 100 pixels**.

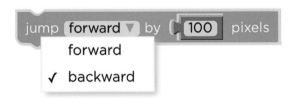

You will notice that many of the blocks have options that you can change. These are called **parameters**, and they let you use one code block in many different ways. The **jump** block has another parameter too: the number of pixels.

6 Let's see what happens when we change more parameters. Change the **jump backward** pixel parameter to "75." Change the **move forward** pixel parameter to "150." Then click **Run**. What happened?

7 Play with your code some more. Experiment by changing parameters and rearranging blocks!

9

Sequence

Olaf can't wait to show off his designs! Look at these drawings. They're created with the same six code blocks. But the blocks appear in a different **sequence**, or order, for each drawing. In your notebook, match the code with the drawing it creates. HINT: Olaf is facing the bottom of the play space at the start of each drawing.

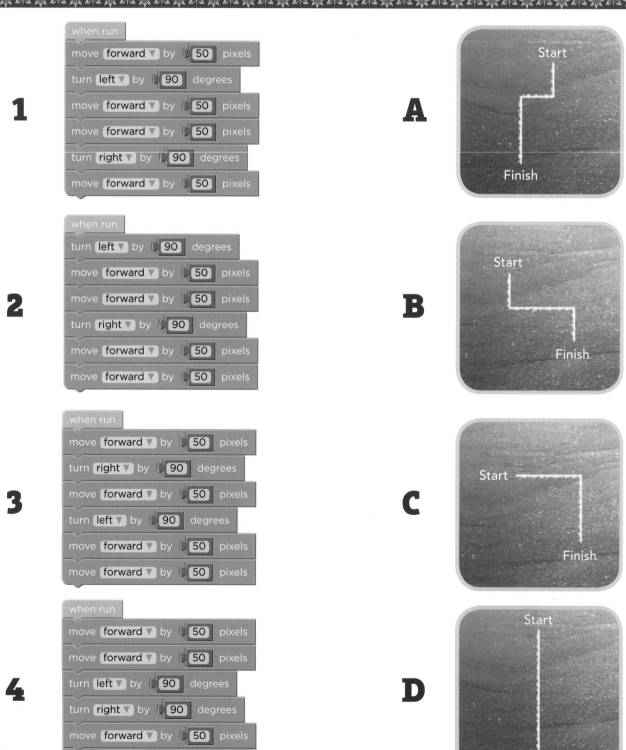

1

```
when run
move forward by 50 pixels
turn left by 90 degrees
move forward by 50 pixels
move forward by 50 pixels
turn right by 90 degrees
move forward by 50 pixels
```

A

Start
Finish

2

```
when run
turn left by 90 degrees
move forward by 50 pixels
move forward by 50 pixels
turn right by 90 degrees
move forward by 50 pixels
move forward by 50 pixels
```

B

Start
Finish

3

```
when run
move forward by 50 pixels
turn right by 90 degrees
move forward by 50 pixels
turn left by 90 degrees
move forward by 50 pixels
move forward by 50 pixels
```

C

Start
Finish

4

```
when run
move forward by 50 pixels
move forward by 50 pixels
turn left by 90 degrees
turn right by 90 degrees
move forward by 50 pixels
move forward by 50 pixels
```

D

Start
Finish

Problem-Solving

Anna draws a maze around Olaf and challenges him to find his way out. Make a copy of this page. Can you help Olaf out of the maze? HINT: Olaf starts off facing the bottom of the play space.

All the blocks needed to solve the maze appear in the program below. But two blocks are in the wrong places! Read through the program line by line. Find the first place where the code goes wrong. What happened? What should have happened? Which block fixes the problem? On your copy of the page, draw stars next to the two blocks that need to be switched.

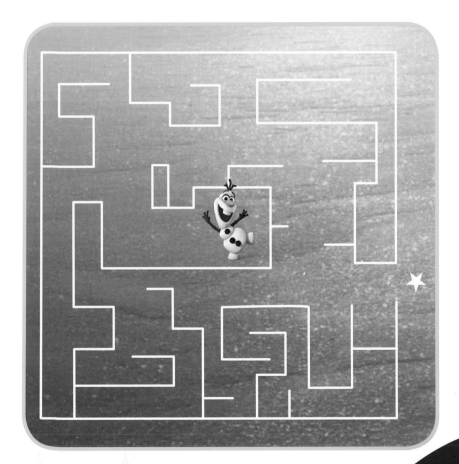

```
when run
turn right by 90 degrees
move forward by 100 pixels
turn right by 90 degrees
move forward by 100 pixels
turn right by 90 degrees
move forward by 100 pixels
turn right by 90 degrees
move forward by 150 pixels
turn left by 90 degrees
move forward by 200 pixels
```

❓ Did You Know?

❄ Every programmer makes mistakes. The important thing is to be able to find and fix them! This process is called **debugging**, because you're getting rid of the problems, or "bugs," in a program.

Draw Squares

Elsa is having a marvelous time creating designs on the ice. Let's help her draw some ice cubes. From the front, an ice cube looks like a simple square. Can you use what you've learned to figure out how to draw a square?

1 Create a new project, and name it "Square."

2 Study this image to figure out what code blocks you'll need to create a square. Plan your program in your notebook.

3 When you're done, build your program online and run it. If the drawing isn't exactly what you expected, don't worry! Just do a little bit of debugging to figure out what went wrong. You'll get it!

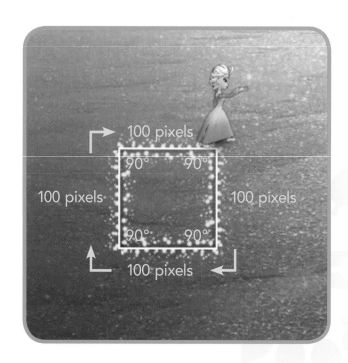

100 pixels
90°   90°
100 pixels   100 pixels
90°   90°
100 pixels

❓ Helpful Tip

✳ When you **remix** a project, it creates a new copy for you to play with. This keeps the code for your original project safe.

4 Now help Elsa draw another square beside the first one. Click on the **Remix** button at the top of the page. This creates a copy of the project. Rename the project "Two Squares." Then add more code blocks by copying the code for the first square. Your program should look like this:

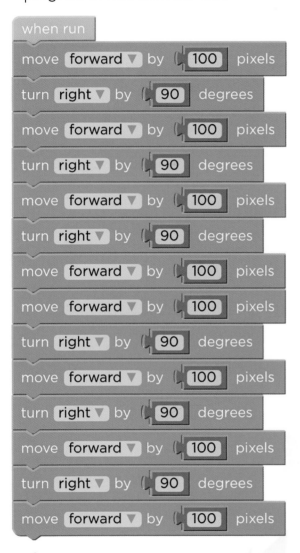

5 Look at your code again. What changes do you need to make to get a drawing that looks like this? HINT: The second square is only 50 pixels long on each side.

6 Where would you need to add a **jump forward by 100 pixels** block to create a drawing like this?

Add a Triangle

Anna loves what Elsa has drawn! She wants to take it a step further by adding a different shape. Let's help her create a design that uses a square and a triangle.

1 Because Anna wants to include a square in her design, let's reuse the code from your "Square" project. First, open your "Square" project. Remix the project, and rename it "Sisters Design."

2 You'll see that your project already has the code needed to draw a square. That's a nice shortcut! Since we are drawing with Anna in this activity, drag the **set character to Anna** block to the workspace. Place it between the **when run** and **move forward** blocks.

3 Now add code blocks to draw a triangle that overlaps the square. Here is an example of how your program could look. Feel free to play around with the parameters. Try making the design bigger or smaller until you're happy with it.

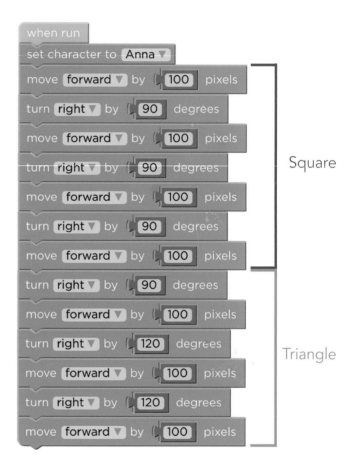

4 A **pattern** is something that repeats. Help Anna create a pattern with her design. Remix and rename your project "Sisters Pattern." How would you change the code if you wanted Anna to draw the design three times?

❓ Did You Know?

✳ An **angle** measure tells us how big or small a turn is. You probably know some information about angles already. Examples might include:

- Each angle in a square measures 90 degrees.
- A straight line measures 180 degrees.
- A circle measures 360 degrees.
- Each angle in an equilateral triangle measures 60 degrees.

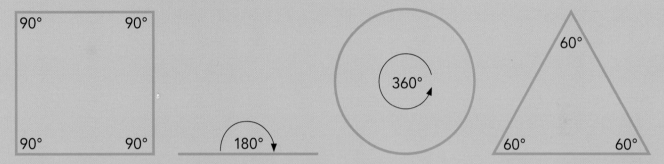

You'll notice that Anna drew an equilateral triangle in the "Sisters Design." Are you wondering why we programmed the turn at 120 degrees instead of 60 degrees? Great question! When Anna and Elsa draw shapes in your programs, they are outside of the shape. This means they draw corners along the outside. They make **exterior angles** for that shape. Exterior angles are different from **interior angles**.

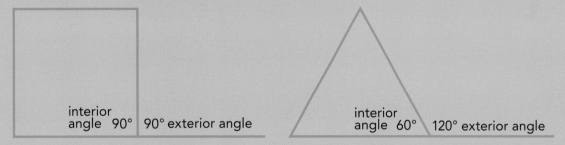

Let's say we want to create a shape with an interior angle of 60 degrees. We have to make a turn of 120 degrees along the outside of that shape. This is because 120 degrees + 60 degrees = 180 degrees. The two angles added together make a straight line, which measures 180 degrees.

Think of it this way: Elsa is walking in a straight line. Then she turns left by 120 degrees and keeps walking. The right side of the angle she just made measures 120 degrees. The left side of the angle measures 60 degrees.

interior angle 60°   120° exterior angle

Debugging

Do you want to draw a snowman? Olaf sure does! But something is not quite right in his drawings. Help Olaf fix the drawings by debugging the code below. Each drawing has something that doesn't belong. Look at the code. Make a copy of this page. Then cross out the block that needs to be removed for the drawing to be correct.

1

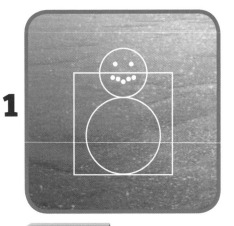

when run
Draw Head
Draw Face
Draw Body
Draw Square

2

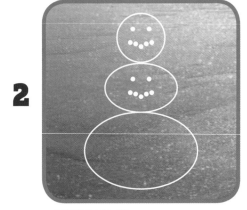

when run
Draw Head
Draw Face
Draw Medium Oval
Draw Face
Draw Large Oval

3

when run
Draw Head
Draw Face
Draw Flower
Draw Oval Body
Draw Feet

4

when run
Draw Head
Draw Face
Draw Large Oval
Draw Medium Oval
Draw Large Oval

Repeat Loops

Anna's designs below use the **repeat loop**. The code inside this block is a **loop** that will run as many times as you tell it to. This makes it easy to do something over and over. In your notebook, match each program with the correct design. HINTS: Anna is facing the bottom of the play space when she starts drawing. Try tracing the design with your finger as you go through the code.

1

```
when run
repeat  4  times
do    move  forward ▼  by  40  pixels
      turn  right ▼  by  90  degrees
      move  forward ▼  by  40  pixels
      turn  left ▼  by  90  degrees
```

A

Start
Finish

2

```
when run
repeat  4  times
do    turn  left ▼  by  90  degrees
      move  forward ▼  by  40  pixels
      turn  right ▼  by  90  degrees
      move  forward ▼  by  40  pixels
```

B

Start
Finish

3

```
when run
repeat  3  times
do    turn  right ▼  by  90  degrees
      move  forward ▼  by  60  pixels
      turn  left ▼  by  90  degrees
      move  forward ▼  by  30  pixels
```

C

Start
Finish

4

```
when run
repeat  3  times
do    move  forward ▼  by  60  pixels
      turn  left ▼  by  90  degrees
      move  forward ▼  by  30  pixels
      turn  right ▼  by  90  degrees
```

D

Start
Finish

17

Patterns That Repeat

Anna enjoys making patterns on the ice. She's thinking about using a stair design to create a diamond pattern.

1 Create a new project, and call it "Diamond Stairs."

2 Start by having Anna jump all the way back to the top left using these blocks.

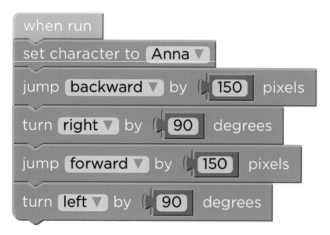

3 Now it's time to create the **repeat** loop that makes one half of the design. Add the code below after the **turn left** block in your workspace. Run the program. The drawing will look like stairs that take Anna from the top of the play space to the bottom.

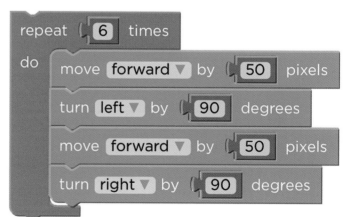

❓ Did You Know?

✳ Loops can save us a lot of work. Imagine if we had to code Anna's staircase design without **repeat** loops. That would mean coding every movement and turn, line by line! Loops give us a powerful shortcut.

4 To finish this design, have Anna turn right by 180 degrees. Then repeat the stair code one more time. Wonderful work!

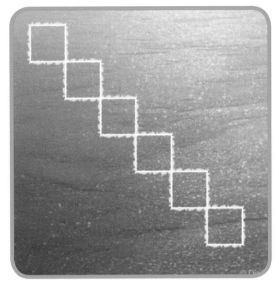

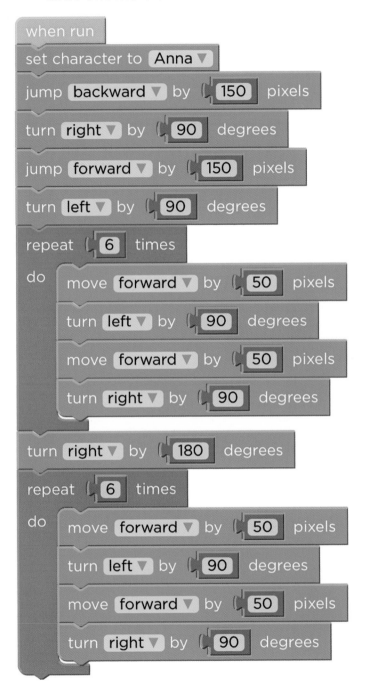

```
when run
set character to  Anna ▼
jump  backward ▼  by  150  pixels
turn  right ▼  by  90  degrees
jump  forward ▼  by  150  pixels
turn  left ▼  by  90  degrees
repeat  6  times
do    move  forward ▼  by  50  pixels
      turn  left ▼  by  90  degrees
      move  forward ▼  by  50  pixels
      turn  right ▼  by  90  degrees

turn  right ▼  by  180  degrees
repeat  6  times
do    move  forward ▼  by  50  pixels
      turn  left ▼  by  90  degrees
      move  forward ▼  by  50  pixels
      turn  right ▼  by  90  degrees
```

Give these extra challenges a try!

- What happens if Anna turns left 180 degrees between **repeat** loops? Why do you think that happens?

- What happens if Anna turns 170 degrees between **repeat** loops?

- Remix your project, and play with your parameters. Try using 80 degrees instead of 90 degrees for each of the stair patterns. Try making each stair step longer or shorter. Try a different starting position for your drawing. Try changing some of the forward/backward and left/right parameters. Try changing the number in the **repeat** loop. Experiment and have fun!

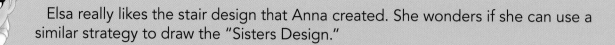

"Sisters Design" with Loops

Elsa really likes the stair design that Anna created. She wonders if she can use a similar strategy to draw the "Sisters Design."

1 Find your "Sisters Design" project. Remix the project and rename it "Sisters Loop."

2 Change the **set character** parameter to "Elsa."

3 Drag a **repeat** loop into the workspace. Change the parameter to "4." Put the first two lines of code for the square inside the loop. Now you can remove the rest of the square code from the workspace.

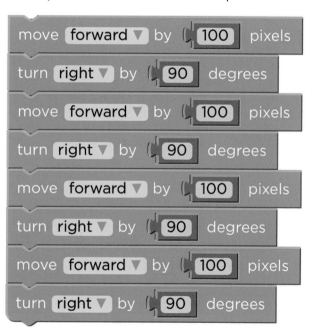

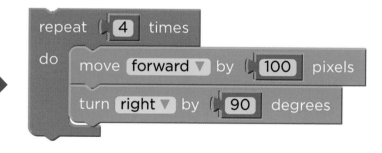

❗ Helpful Tip

❄ Click on the **My Projects** button to see a list of your saved projects. The button is located in the top right corner of the page.

20

4 Drag another **repeat** loop into the workspace. Change the parameter to "3." Put the first two lines of code for the triangle inside the loop. Then remove the rest of the triangle code.

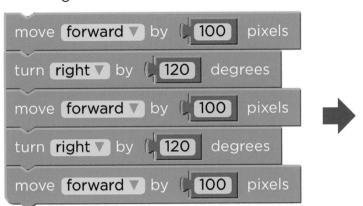

5 Click your two **repeat** loops into place under the **set character** block. Your program will look like this:

```
when run
set character to Elsa ▼
repeat    4    times
do    move forward ▼ by   100   pixels
      turn right ▼ by   90   degrees
repeat    3    times
do    move forward ▼ by   100   pixels
      turn right ▼ by   120   degrees
```

Now run your code. You'll see that Elsa's design is the same as Anna's from page 14. You'll also notice that using the **repeat** loops saves us from writing several extra lines of code. These loops are really useful!

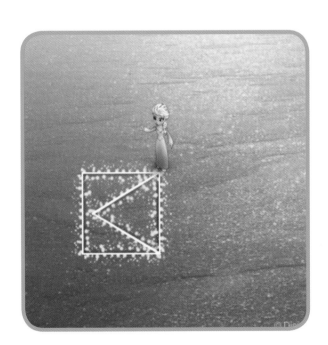

❓ Did You Know?

❄ Even when they create the same design, Elsa's and Anna's drawings look slightly different. This is because they each have a unique drawing style. Elsa creates her drawings with ice magic, and Anna creates hers with ice skates.

Nested Loops

Seeing Elsa work with the "Sisters Design" has given Anna an idea. She thinks it could be used to make a beautiful snowflake!

1 What happens if you put a loop inside of another loop? This is called a **nested loop**, and it can help you create some amazing drawings. Let's try it! First, remix your "Sisters Loop" project and call it "Sisters Nested Loop."

2 Change the **set character** parameter to "Anna." Then add a **turn right** block to the end of your code. Change the degree parameter to "60."

3 Drag a **repeat** loop into the workspace, and change the parameter to "6." Put the **repeat** loop directly under the **set character** block. Then drag the remaining code blocks inside the **repeat** loop.

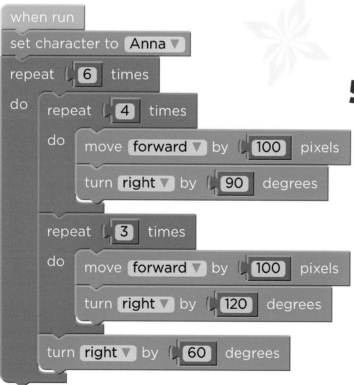

4 When you click **Run**, Anna will draw the "Sisters" pattern six times with a turn of 60 degrees between each one. That's an interesting snowflake you've helped Anna make!

5 What do you need to change if you want to repeat the "Sisters" pattern seven, eight, or nine times?

❓ Did You Know?

❇ It's not hard to figure out how many degrees you need to spin a shape in order to take it around in a full circle. All you need is a little math!

- Figure out how many times you want the shape to go around.

- Divide 360 degrees (the number of degrees in a circle) by that number. The result is the number of degrees you need to turn!

Take, for example, the snowflake Anna drew using the "Sisters Design." She spun the design around 6 times. 360 degrees ÷ 6 = 60 degrees. That is why we used 60 degrees in our code.

Look at Elsa's design below. It uses 8 squares. 360 degrees ÷ 8 = 45 degrees. This means we need to turn 45 degrees after drawing each square.

```
when run
set character to Elsa ▽
repeat   8   times
do    repeat   4   times
      do    move forward ▽ by  100  pixels
            turn right ▽ by  90  degrees
      turn right ▽ by  45  degrees
```

❇ How many degrees would we use if we wanted to spin the square around 10 times? Complete this equation in your notebook to find the answer:

360 degrees ÷ _____ = _____

```
when run
set character to Elsa ▽
repeat   10   times
do    repeat   4   times
      do    move forward ▽ by  100  pixels
            turn right ▽ by  90  degrees
      turn right ▽ by  ??  degrees
```

23

Nested Designs

Olaf is inspired by Anna and Elsa. He wants to create some cool designs of his own. Make a copy of this page. The drawings below use nested loops. How many times do you need to repeat each block of code to get each image?

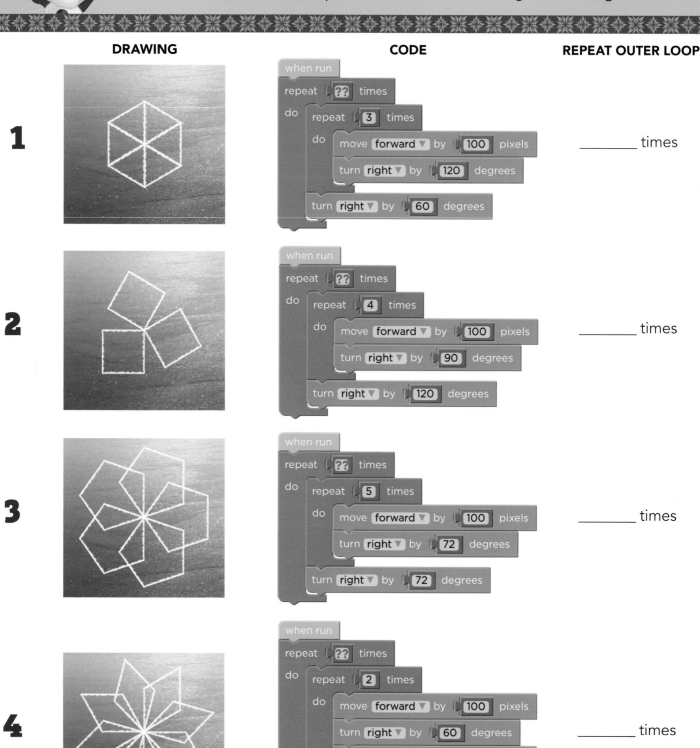

	DRAWING	CODE	REPEAT OUTER LOOP

1

```
when run
repeat [??] times
do   repeat [3] times
     do   move forward by [100] pixels
          turn right by [120] degrees
     turn right by [60] degrees
```

_____ times

2

```
when run
repeat [??] times
do   repeat [4] times
     do   move forward by [100] pixels
          turn right by [90] degrees
     turn right by [120] degrees
```

_____ times

3

```
when run
repeat [??] times
do   repeat [5] times
     do   move forward by [100] pixels
          turn right by [72] degrees
     turn right by [72] degrees
```

_____ times

4

```
when run
repeat [??] times
do   repeat [2] times
     do   move forward by [100] pixels
          turn right by [60] degrees
          move forward by [100] pixels
          turn right by [120] degrees
     turn right by [45] degrees
```

_____ times

Functions

Loops are great when you want to repeat the same actions many times in a row. But what if you want to do other things in between? That's when you use a **function**. This is a function block.

`do something`

You can put code in it the same way that you put code into a **repeat** loop. The difference is that each function has its own name, and you can **call a function** from anywhere in your program!

Use functions to help Elsa draw a series of shapes. In your notebook, write the functions in the correct order to create this design. HINT: Elsa will draw the shapes from left to right.

These are the functions you will call:

`Draw Circle`

`Draw Diamond`

`Draw Star`

Draw Flowers with Functions

The people of Arendelle love flowers, even in winter! Anna wants to draw a big bouquet to show how much she appreciates everyone in the kingdom. Can you help her?

Flowers can be difficult to draw, and they can take a lot of code to create. It would be frustrating to have to write all that code every time you wanted to make another flower. Now you can use functions to save your code. That way, you can make as many flowers as you like just by calling the function!

1 Create a new project, and call it "Flower." Add the **set character to Anna** block.

2 Go to the toolbox under **Functions**, and click the orange **Create a Function** button.

Create a Function

3 A new window called the **function editor** will appear. Here, you can name your function and describe what it does. There is also an area to **define the function** by dropping in code, the same way you do in the workspace.

4 Name your function something that clearly states what it will do, like "Draw Flower."

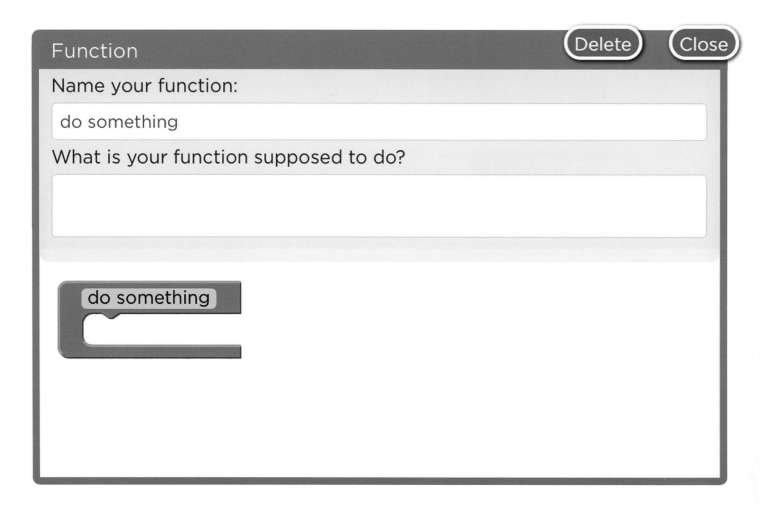

5 Put all the code for your flower inside the green block in the function editor. You can make up your own, or you can use code like this:

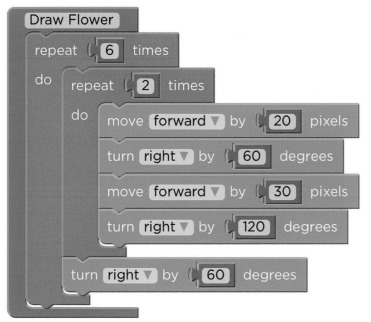

Click **Close** to exit the function editor.

6 Back in your main window, look under the **Functions** label in the toolbox. Find the **Draw Flower** block that has now appeared. Drag that block into the workspace under the **set character** block.

7 Run your program. What does your flower look like? If you aren't happy with it, click the **edit** button in your **Draw Flower** function block. Try changing some of the parameters. You can keep editing your function until you're happy with your flower design.

8 Ready to see the power of functions? Let's move Anna around the play space with the **jump** blocks and call the function many times. Try using **repeat** loops or even nested loops! Try to fill the play space with flowers. Can you create a drawing that looks like this?

Experiment and come up with your own design and code! (Check out the Answer Key to see the code that created the drawing above.)

❗ Helpful Tips

✳ If you run your program while you're creating your function for the first time, it won't work. That's because the **Run** button doesn't run what you see in the function editor. It runs the program connected to the **when run** block in the main workspace. To see your function run, close the function editor and add your **function call** block to the main program.

✳ Want to change the code for a function? Click the blue **edit** button on the **function call** block. This will open the function editor again.

More Flowers with Functions

The children of Arendelle have joined Anna in drawing flowers on the ice. They're creating a beautiful garden of ice flowers! Help Anna and the children fill their garden with different flowers by creating more functions.

1 Remix your "Flower" project, and rename it "More Flowers."

2 Follow the directions from the last activity to make three more flower functions. Call them "Draw Flower 2," "Draw Flower 3," and "Draw Flower 4." You can create your own code, or create functions like these:

```
Draw Flower 2
repeat [ 8 ] times
do    repeat [ 3 ] times
      do    move forward ▼ by [ 40 ] pixels
            turn right ▼ by [ 120 ] degrees
      turn right ▼ by [ 45 ] degrees
```

```
Draw Flower 3
repeat [ 5 ] times
do    repeat [ 4 ] times
      do    move forward ▼ by [ 40 ] pixels
            turn right ▼ by [ 90 ] degrees
      turn right ▼ by [ 72 ] degrees
```

```
Draw Flower 4
repeat [ 4 ] times
do    repeat [ 6 ] times
      do    move forward ▼ by [ 15 ] pixels
            turn right ▼ by [ 60 ] degrees
      turn right ▼ by [ 90 ] degrees
```

3 Once you have all four of your flower functions defined, go back to your main program.

Adjust the code so that you call each of the flower functions. Try to create something like this:

(Check out the Answer Key to see the code that created the drawing above.)

4 Experiment and fill the play space with different flowers!

❗ Helpful Tip

❄ Loops will come in handy if you'd like to draw curves for your flower designs. To draw a curve, move 1 pixel and turn 1 degree with each loop. Repeating your loop 180 times will give you a half circle. To draw a full circle, repeat your loop 360 times.

Nested Functions

Elsa looks down and sees two different flowers drawn in the same spot. The combined design looks like a glistening snowflake! Help Elsa draw flower snowflakes by using functions inside another function! These are called **nested functions**.

1 Remix your "More Flowers" project, and rename it "Flower Snowflakes."

2 Change the **set character** parameter to "Elsa."

3 Under the **Functions** label in the toolbox, click the **Create a Function** button.

4 In the function editor, name your function "Draw Flower Snowflake." Drag two of your flower functions into your "Draw Flower Snowflake" function. For example,

Close the function editor.

5 Back in the workspace, remove all code after the **set character** block.

6 Add the **Draw Flower Snowflake** block under the **set character** block. Run the program. What does your flower snowflake look like? Add code to your program to fill the play space with flower snowflakes!

7 Remix your project, and rename it "More Flower Snowflakes."

8 Create more flower snowflake functions. Page 31 shows some of Elsa's flower combinations. Can you create some similar designs? HINT: Refer to the code on page 28. Adjust the parameters until you're happy with the design. Then think of different ways to combine your flower functions into flower snowflake functions.

9 Create a program that calls all your flower snowflake functions. Fill the play space with your designs. Does it look as though there's a blizzard in Arendelle?

Simplifying with Functions

One way to simplify a program is to look for repeating code that can be pulled out into a function. Study this program. Find the section of code that repeats. In your notebook, write a function name for this code. Then write the simplified program using functions.

```
when run
jump to (100) over (100) down
turn (left ▼) by (140) degrees
repeat (2) times
do
    move (forward ▼) by (50) pixels
    turn (left ▼) by (80) degrees
    move (forward ▼) by (50) pixels
    turn (left ▼) by (100) degrees

turn (right ▼) by (50) degrees
jump to (200) over (200) down
turn (left ▼) by (50) degrees
repeat (2) times
do
    move (forward ▼) by (50) pixels
    turn (left ▼) by (80) degrees
    move (forward ▼) by (50) pixels
    turn (left ▼) by (100) degrees

turn (right ▼) by (50) degrees
jump to (300) over (300) down
turn (left ▼) by (50) degrees
repeat (2) times
do
    move (forward ▼) by (50) pixels
    turn (left ▼) by (80) degrees
    move (forward ▼) by (50) pixels
    turn (left ▼) by (100) degrees
```

For Loops

Now it's time to learn about **for loops**! These loops use a **counter** to go from a **starting value** to an **ending value** by an **increment**.

This program uses a **for** loop to draw dots in a spiral. See how it starts by drawing one dot, ends by drawing three dots, and adds one dot each time through?

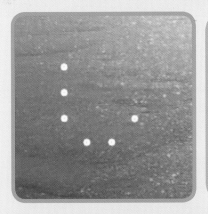

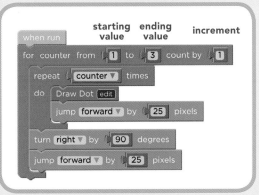

The drawings below all use the code from this program. The only differences are the parameters used in the **for** loop. In your notebook, fill in the **for** loop to get each drawing shown. HINTS: Count the dots on each side of the spiral. Each drawing starts at the center of the spiral.

1

for counter from _____ to

_____ count by _____

2

for counter from _____ to

_____ count by _____

3

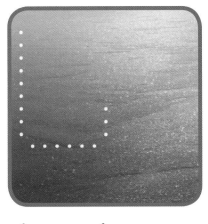

for counter from _____ to

_____ count by _____

4

for counter from _____ to

_____ count by _____

For Loop Spirals

Elsa is practicing her spirals. The ice looks quite elegant covered in swirls! Do you want to help her create an amazing design using a **for** loop? Let's try it!

1 Create a new project, and call it "Square Spiral."

2 Drag a **for** loop into the workspace and click it into place under the **when run** block. You will find the **for** loop block under the **Loops** label in the toolbox.

3 Next, drag a **move forward** block and a **turn right** block into the **for** loop.

4 Grab the purple number block inside the **move forward** block, and drag it back to the toolbox.

5 Find the **counter** block under the **Variables** label in the toolbox. Drag it into the **move forward** block. This tells Elsa to move the same amount as your counter every time through the loop.

6 Finally, set the **for** loop's starting value to "5" and ending value to "300." Set the increment to "5." Here's what the completed code looks like:

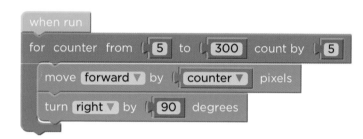

7 Click **Run** to see what happens. What an amazing drawing!

8 Time to play around with your code! Remix your project, and rename it "Square Spiral 2." Let's say you want more space between the lines of your spiral. No problem! Just change the parameters in the **for** loop. Set the start value to "10" and the increment to "10." How do you like this spiral?

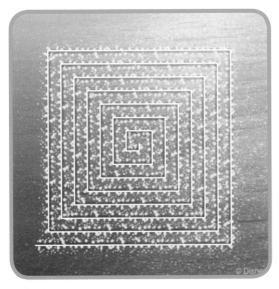

9 Can you figure out what code block to add to your program to create this drawing? That's right! Just add a **turn right** block before the **for** loop and set the degree parameter to "45."

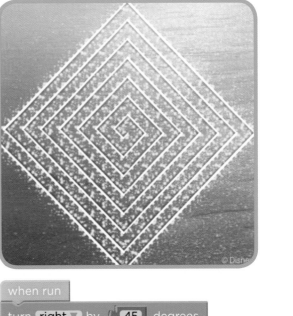

10 Play with the parameters, and create your own spiral designs.

? Did You Know?

✳ Like **repeat** loops, **for** loops are a powerful tool. With just a few lines of code, you can create intricate drawings like the spirals shown here. Can you think of other ways to use a **for** loop?

More Spiral Designs

Anna wants to try something different with Elsa's spiral design. She wonders how to make spirals that are not perfectly square. Use your coding skills to help Anna create a unique design!

1 Remix your "Square Spiral" project, and call it "More Spirals."

2 Add the **set character to Anna** block between the **when run** block and the **for** loop.

3 Instead of turning right by 90 degrees, try a slightly different angle.

4 Play around with the degree parameter until you have a design you like.

5 Next, try changing the color of your lines to give your spiral more personality! You can find the **set color** block under the **Actions** label in the toolbox.

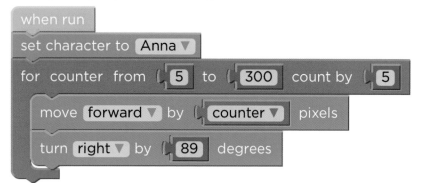

```
when run
set character to Anna ▼
for counter from ( 5 ) to ( 300 ) count by ( 5 )
    move forward ▼ by ( counter ▼ ) pixels
    turn right ▼ by ( 89 ) degrees
```

These drawings use 89 degrees and 91 degrees, respectively. Look at how different these drawings are from Elsa's spiral. And the only change was a 1-degree difference in each turn!

6 Now change the increment parameter in the **for** loop. What happens when you make the increment bigger or smaller? Here are some examples of spiral designs you can try:

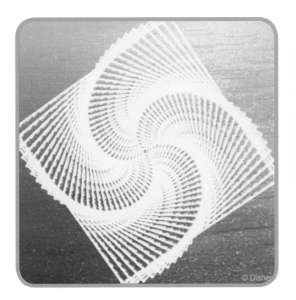

```
when run
set character to  Anna ▼
set color  ⬜
for  counter  from  5  to  300  count by  2
    move  forward ▼  by  counter ▼  pixels
    turn  right ▼  by  91  degrees
```

```
when run
set character to  Anna ▼
set color  ⬜
for  counter  from  3  to  300  count by  3
    move  forward ▼  by  counter ▼  pixels
    turn  right ▼  by  93  degrees
```

7 Experiment until you're happy with your unique spiral design.

A Grand Snowflake

As the people of Arendelle enjoy drawing on the ice, snowflakes begin to drift down from the sky. The gentle snowfall inspires Elsa to draw an intricate snowflake design.

Help Elsa create a design that uses overlapping shapes of different sizes. Think back to when you made shapes and spun them around in a circle. **For** loops will let you do that in many sizes. Give it a try!

1 Create a new project, and name it "Grand Snowflake."

2 Add the code below to your workspace. Click **Run** to see Elsa draw a snowflake made of different-sized pentagons. How lovely!

```
when run
for counter from ( 100 ) to ( 25 ) count by ( 25 )
    set color ( random color
    repeat ( 5 ) times
    do  repeat ( 5 ) times
        do  move forward ▼ by ( counter ▼ ) pixels
            turn left ▼ by ( 72 ) degrees
        turn right ▼ by ( 72 ) degrees
```

3 Perhaps you'd like the snowflake to be made from a different shape. You can just as easily use triangles, squares, hexagons, or even octagons! Just change the parameters for the innermost loop to make a new shape.

NUMBER OF SIDES	CODE

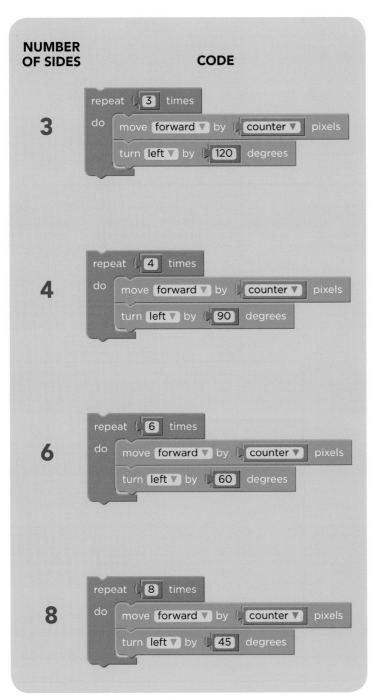

3
```
repeat [ 3 ] times
do    move  forward ▼  by  [ counter ▼ ]  pixels
      turn  left ▼  by  [ 120 ]  degrees
```

4
```
repeat [ 4 ] times
do    move  forward ▼  by  [ counter ▼ ]  pixels
      turn  left ▼  by  [ 90 ]  degrees
```

6
```
repeat [ 6 ] times
do    move  forward ▼  by  [ counter ▼ ]  pixels
      turn  left ▼  by  [ 60 ]  degrees
```

8
```
repeat [ 8 ] times
do    move  forward ▼  by  [ counter ▼ ]  pixels
      turn  left ▼  by  [ 45 ]  degrees
```

4 Let's say you want to change how many times a shape is drawn each time the **for** loop runs. Which parameters would you need to change?

HINTS: There are two parameters you need to adjust. The code on page 38 draws the shape five times in each iteration of the **for** loop.

Follow the Code

Olaf, Anna, and Elsa are having so much fun on the ice that they accidentally draw over one another's designs. Oh dear!

This drawing is made up of three different designs. Can you figure out which part of the drawing is made by Olaf? Look at the code for Olaf's design, shown as a function below. Copy this page, and draw his design in the empty box. HINTS: The dot in the middle of the box shows where Olaf is standing before he begins drawing. He is facing the bottom of the play space.

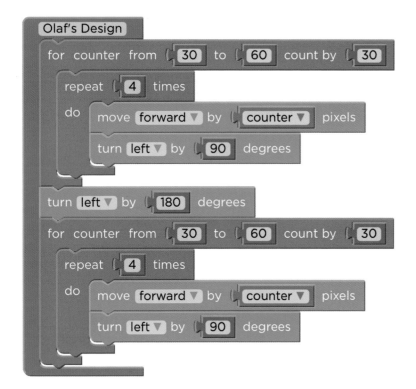

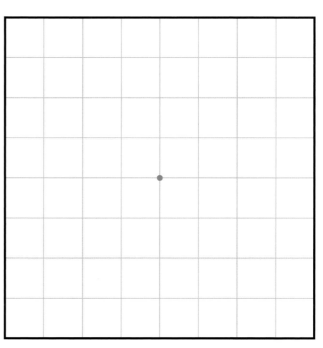

Each grid box represents 30 pixels across and 30 pixels down.

The sun is hanging low in the sky as the ice-drawing event comes to an end. Elsa, Anna, and Olaf work with the people of Arendelle to create one final drawing. Everyone has had a great time today. They know they'll remember this wonderful day for a long time to come.

You should be proud of everything you've learned! Now it's time to review the ideas that you've explored in this book. Look at the code used to create the drawing below. Copy this page, and complete the following tasks.

1 Draw an arrow pointing to the **repeat** loop in this code.

2 Draw a triangle next to the **for** loop.

3 Draw a star next to the **function call** block.

4 Draw a check mark on top of the increment in the **for** loop.

5 Draw rectangles around all the parameters in this program.

```
when run
for counter from [ 15 ] to [ 140 ] count by [ 5 ]
    jump  forward ▼  by [ counter ▼ ] pixels
    turn  left ▼  by [ 45 ] degrees
    set color [ random color ]
    repeat [ 5 ] times
    do   jump  forward ▼  by [ 8 ] pixels
         Draw Dot  edit
         jump  backward ▼  by [ 8 ] pixels
         turn  left ▼  by [ 72 ] degrees
```

© Disney

Get Inspired!

Congratulations on your adventures in coding! Let's see what creative drawings you can make using a handful of code blocks.

Make a copy of these pages. Each activity below presents five code blocks. Include them in your own program to create a special drawing. You can arrange the blocks in any way you like. Feel free to include other code blocks too. Adjust the code until you're happy with your drawing. When you're done, draw the image your code created.

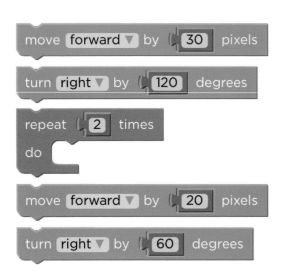

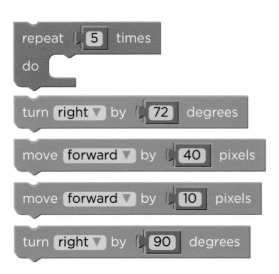

for counter from `30` to `60` count by `30`

move `forward ▼` by `counter ▼` pixels

turn `left ▼` by `90` degrees

repeat `4` times
do

turn `left ▼` by `45` degrees

for counter from `100` to `25` count by `25`

set color `random color`

move `forward ▼` by `counter ▼` pixels

repeat `6` times
do

turn `left ▼` by `60` degrees

jump `backward ▼` by `25` pixels

create a circle
        size: `counter ▼`

turn `right ▼` by `30` degrees

set color `random color`

for counter from `1` to `12` count by `1`

Try It Yourself!

As you've learned, you can do some amazing things with code. Are you ready for more coding challenges? Look at the pictures below, and try to write code that draws something similar. Then experiment with the ideas you've explored in this book and create some drawings all on your own. Make a copy of page 45 to plan a project to share with family and friends!

1

2

3

4

Answer Key

PAGE 10
1. B
2. C
3. A
4. D

PAGE 11

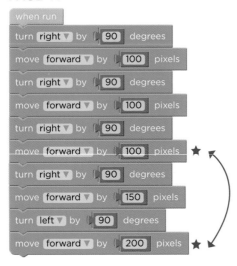

```
when run
turn right ▼ by [ 90 ] degrees
move forward ▼ by [ 100 ] pixels
turn right ▼ by [ 90 ] degrees
move forward ▼ by [ 100 ] pixels
turn right ▼ by [ 90 ] degrees
move forward ▼ by [ 100 ] pixels   ★
turn right ▼ by [ 90 ] degrees
move forward ▼ by [ 150 ] pixels
turn left ▼ by [ 90 ] degrees
move forward ▼ by [ 200 ] pixels   ★
```

PAGE 16

1.
```
when run
Draw Head
Draw Face
Draw Body
Draw Square
```

2.
```
when run
Draw Head
Draw Face
Draw Medium Oval
Draw Face
Draw Large Oval
```

3.
```
when run
Draw Head
Draw Face
Draw Flower
Draw Oval Body
Draw Feet
```

4.
```
when run
Draw Head
Draw Face
Draw Large Oval
Draw Medium Oval
Draw Large Oval
```

PAGE 17
1. C
2. A
3. D
4. B

PAGE 24
1. 6
2. 3
3. 5
4. 8

PAGE 25
when run
Draw Diamond
Draw Diamond
Draw Circle
Draw Star
Draw Circle
Draw Diamond
Draw Diamond

PAGE 27

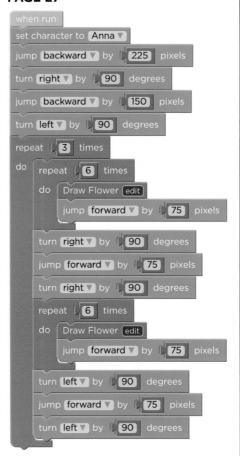

```
when run
set character to [ Anna ▼ ]
jump backward ▼ by [ 225 ] pixels
turn right ▼ by [ 90 ] degrees
jump backward ▼ by [ 150 ] pixels
turn left ▼ by [ 90 ] degrees
repeat [ 3 ] times
do   repeat [ 6 ] times
     do   Draw Flower [edit]
          jump forward ▼ by [ 75 ] pixels
     turn right ▼ by [ 90 ] degrees
     jump forward ▼ by [ 75 ] pixels
     turn right ▼ by [ 90 ] degrees
     repeat [ 6 ] times
     do   Draw Flower [edit]
          jump forward ▼ by [ 75 ] pixels
     turn left ▼ by [ 90 ] degrees
     jump forward ▼ by [ 75 ] pixels
     turn left ▼ by [ 90 ] degrees
```

PAGE 29

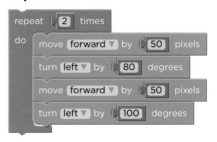

```
when run
set character to [ Anna ▼ ]
jump backward ▼ by [ 150 ] pixels
turn right ▼ by [ 90 ] degrees
jump forward ▼ by [ 75 ] pixels
turn left ▼ by [ 90 ] degrees
repeat [ 2 ] times
do   Draw Flower [edit]
     jump forward ▼ by [ 100 ] pixels
     Draw Flower 2 [edit]
     jump forward ▼ by [ 100 ] pixels
     Draw Flower 3 [edit]
     jump forward ▼ by [ 100 ] pixels
     Draw Flower 4 [edit]
     turn left ▼ by [ 90 ] degrees
     jump forward ▼ by [ 150 ] pixels
     turn left ▼ by [ 90 ] degrees
```

PAGE 32

Repeated Code

```
repeat [ 2 ] times
do   move forward ▼ by [ 50 ] pixels
     turn left ▼ by [ 80 ] degrees
     move forward ▼ by [ 50 ] pixels
     turn left ▼ by [ 100 ] degrees
```

Name Your Function
Draw Diamond*

Simplified Program
when run
jump to 100 over 100 down
turn left by 140 degrees
Draw Diamond
turn right by 50 degrees
jump to 200 over 200 down
turn left by 50 degrees
Draw Diamond
turn right by 50 degrees
jump to 300 over 300 down
turn left by 50 degrees
Draw Diamond

PAGE 33

1. for counter from **1** to **5** count by **1**
2. for counter from **2** to **8** count by **2**
3. for counter from **3** to **9** count by **3**
4. for counter from **1** to **7** count by **1**

PAGE 40

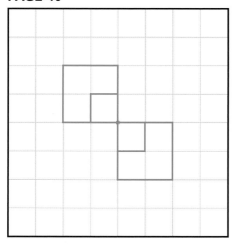

PAGE 41

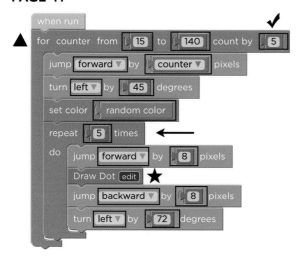

* You may have given the function a different name. As long as your function calls match your function name, the program will work.

PAGE 44

1.
```
when run
jump backward ▼ by  150  pixels
turn left ▼ by  90  degrees
jump backward ▼ by  10  pixels
set color  [  ]
create a circle
        size:  25
```

2.
```
when run
set character to Anna ▼
jump forward ▼ by  25  pixels
turn right ▼ by  90  degrees
for counter from  0  to  360  count by  15
    move forward ▼ by  counter ▼  pixels
    turn right ▼ by  120  degrees
```

3.
```
when run
repeat  6  times
do  set color  random color
    repeat  2  times
    do  move forward ▼ by  75  pixels
        turn right ▼ by  45  degrees
        move forward ▼ by  75  pixels
        turn right ▼ by  135  degrees
    turn right ▼ by  60  degrees
```

4.
```
when run
set character to Anna ▼
turn left ▼ by  90  degrees
for counter from  8  to  152  count by  8
    set color  [  ]
    move forward ▼ by  counter ▼  pixels
    turn left ▼ by  60  degrees
    set color  random color
    repeat  5  times
    do  jump forward ▼ by  4  pixels
        Draw Dot [edit]
        jump backward ▼ by  4  pixels
        turn left ▼ by  72  degrees

Draw Dot
create a circle
        size:  0.3
```

47

Glossary

angle:
The number of degrees that a line turns at a corner.

block-based language:
A programming language that runs programs that have been created using code blocks that resemble puzzle pieces.

Blockly:
A visual programming language that lets you drag and drop code to create programs.

call a function:
To ask the computer to run the code inside a function.

code:
Instructions for a computer.

coding:
The process of creating code.

computer science:
The study of computers and computer-related ideas.

counter:
A placeholder that keeps track of a value that is added to (or subtracted from) each time through a for loop.

debugging:
Finding and fixing errors in a program.

define the function:
To put code inside a function block that tells the computer what to do when that function is called inside a program.

ending value:
The value where your counter will stop counting in a for loop.

exterior angles:
The measurements of the outside of an angle.

for loops:
Loops where you can control the starting value, ending value, and increment.

function:
A named piece of code that you can call in a program whenever you need it.

function editor:
A pop-up box that lets you create or edit the code inside your function.

increment:
The amount that your counter goes up (or down) each time through a for loop.

interior angles:
The measurements of an angle from the inside of the shape.

loop:
A segment of code that runs over and over without doing anything else in between.

nested functions:
Functions placed inside other functions.

nested loop:
A loop placed inside another loop.

parameters:
Special places where you can customize certain blocks to do things in different ways.

pattern:
Something that repeats multiple times.

pixels:
Small squares laid out in a grid that make up an image. A pixel can also be a unit of measurement used to specify how far along that grid something travels.

play space:
The area of the website where you see what your code does when it runs.

program:
A set of instructions for a computer.

remix:
To save a copy of a program so you can build it into something new. This allows you to use functions and sections of code you've already created, instead of rebuilding them from scratch.

repeat loop:
The block that allows you to loop a code sequence as many times as you tell it to.

sequence:
The order in which things are arranged.

software:
Programs that run on a machine or computer.

starting value:
The value where your counter will start counting in a for loop.

toolbox:
The area of the website where you find the code blocks to create your program.

workspace:
The area of the website where you drag code to create a program.